FEARLESS
FUNDRAISING
FOR NONPROFIT BOARDS

BY WORTH GEORGE

REVISED EDITION

BOARDSOURCE
Building Effective Nonprofit Boards

Formerly the National Center for Nonprofit Boards

Library of Congress Cataloging-in-Publication Data

George, Worth
    Fearless fundraising for nonprofit boards /

Worth George — Rev. ed.
    p. cm.

Includes bibliographical references.
    ISBN 1-58686-065-8 (pbk.)

1. Fund raising.
2. Nonprofit organizations—Finance.
I. Title.
    HV41.2 .W67 2003
    658.15'224—dc21

2002015382

Formerly the National Center for Nonprofit Boards

BoardSource, formerly the National Center for Nonprofit Boards, is the premier resource for practical information, tools and best practices, training, and leadership development for board members of nonprofit organizations worldwide. Through our highly acclaimed programs and services, BoardSource enables organizations to fulfill their missions by helping build strong and effective nonprofit boards.

BoardSource provides assistance and resources to nonprofit leaders through workshops, training, and our extensive Web site, www.boardsource.org. A team of BoardSource governance consultants works directly with nonprofit leaders to design specialized solutions to meet organizations' needs and assists nongovernmental organizations around the world through partnerships and capacity building. As the world's largest, most comprehensive publisher of materials on nonprofit governance, BoardSource offers a wide selection of books, videotapes, and CDs. BoardSource also hosts the National Leadership Forum, bringing together approximately 800 governance experts, board members, and chief executives of nonprofit organizations from around the world.

Created out of the nonprofit sector's critical need for governance guidance and expertise, BoardSource is a 501(c)(3) nonprofit organization that has provided practical solutions to nonprofit organizations of all sizes in diverse communities. In 2001, BoardSource changed its name from the National Center for Nonprofit Boards to better reflect its mission. Today, BoardSource has more than 15,000 members and has served more than 75,000 nonprofit leaders.

For more information, please visit our Web site at www.boardsource.org, e-mail us at mail@boardsource.org, or call us at 800-883-6262.

HAVE YOU USED THESE BOARDSOURCE RESOURCES?

VIDEOS

Meeting the Challenge: An Orientation to Nonprofit Board Service

Speaking of Money: A Guide to Fund-Raising for Nonprofit Board Members

Building a Successful Team: A Guide to Nonprofit Board Development

BOOKS

The Board Chair Handbook

Managing Conflicts of Interest: Practical Guidelines for Nonprofit Boards

Checks and Balances: The Board Member's Guide to Nonprofit Financial Audits

The Board-Savvy CEO: How To Build a Strong, Positive Relationship with Your Board

Presenting: Board Orientation

Presenting: Fund-Raising

Presenting: Nonprofit Financials

The Board Meeting Rescue Kit: 20 Ideas for Jumpstarting Your Board Meetings

The Board Building Cycle: Nine Steps to Finding, Recruiting, and Engaging Nonprofit Board Members

The Policy Sampler: A Resource for Nonprofit Boards

To Go Forward, Retreat! The Board Retreat Handbook

Nonprofit Board Answer Book: Practical Guide for Board Members and Chief Executives

Nonprofit Board Answer Book II: Beyond the Basics

The Legal Obligations of Nonprofit Boards

Self-Assessment for Nonprofit Governing Boards

Assessment of the Chief Executive

The Nonprofit Board's Guide to Bylaws

Creating and Using Investment Policies

Transforming Board Structure: New Possibilities for Committees and Task Forces

THE GOVERNANCE SERIES

1. Ten Basic Responsibilities of Nonprofit Boards

2. Financial Responsibilities of Nonprofit Boards

3. Structures and Practices of Nonprofit Boards

4. Fundraising Responsibilities of Nonprofit Boards

5. Legal Responsibilities of Nonprofit Boards

6. The Nonprofit Board's Role in Setting and Advancing the Mission

7. The Nonprofit Board's Role in Planning and Evaluation

8. How To Help Your Board Govern More and Manage Less

9. Leadership Roles in Nonprofit Governance

For an up-to-date list of publications and information about current prices, membership, and other services, please call BoardSource at 800-883-6262 or visit our Web site at www.boardsource.org.

Each board member must find what part he or she can play. Let members start by doing what they enjoy most and are good at — thus nurtured and led, board members come to accept broader responsibility for participating in fund-raising [sic] activities and to overcome their understandable resistance.

— Fisher Howe in *The Board Member's Guide to Fund Raising*

Contents

Introduction

Board leadership and participation are essential to successful fundraising. Raising money also requires a great deal of work and a true partnership between board members and key staff. Board members' roles are multi-faceted — they serve not only as strategists and policy makers, but also as individual solicitors. As board members attempt to ensure that the organization has sufficient resources to implement its mission, their personal involvement in fundraising becomes critical.

For many, this is a daunting prospect. Despite their professional skills, enthusiasm about the mission, knowledge of community needs, and problem-solving abilities, very few individuals come to board service equipped with development skills. Even learning how to raise money is frustrating, since the activity is often unclear. Similarly, board members sometimes try to do too much too soon. Asking untrained, ill-prepared board members to make one-on-one solicitation calls is a disservice to everyone involved. Not only are they likely to fail, but an initial negative experience may discourage future involvement.

The lack of specific fundraising training is a persistent problem among boards. Providing concrete examples of how board members can be involved will make them more likely contributors to the organization's development program. Also, when board members' fundraising efforts begin slowly and increase in complexity over time, they raise money more confidently and effectively.

ASKING FOR MONEY

Board members who are ill trained can appear hesitant when asking for money. Nothing could be worse. An apologetic ask is an invitation to failure. By asking for a charitable gift, board members offer donors an opportunity to invest, to give back, and to make a difference. Being vague or unwilling to get to the punch line helps no one, confuses the prospect, and diminishes the cause.

The natural apprehension about solicitation underscores why it's important that board members be trained in the art of fundraising. A board member becomes a fearless fundraiser over time. It will be a while before you're comfortable asking for money for your organization. But this book gives you the right skills to grow steadily more confident.

In their book *The Aladdin Factor,* authors Jack Canfield and Mark Victor Hansen point out that rejection is an illusion. "If you didn't have it before you asked for it, you haven't really lost anything. You are not worse off. [By not] asking, you already have failed. That's more of a defeat than having asked and been turned down." This insight may help volunteer leaders who are anxious about turndowns.

"How Tos"

Giving board members choices, options, and specific instructions enables them to become proficient fundraisers. This new clarity about fundraising may energize and motivate some individuals to do much more than they originally thought possible. A handful may evolve into leaders. Increased board member involvement in fundraising not only helps the organization's development efforts, it also leads to greater board member satisfaction and commitment.

This book offers specific instruction and activities to encourage fearless fundraising. The material is intended to help chief executives, board chairs, and heads of development committees as they guide their fellow board members toward increased participation. First, the book establishes the importance of board involvement — framing development as a top priority. Next, it addresses why and when donors are likely to give. Finally, the book shows chief executives and board chairs how to motivate board members and lead them to greater involvement in fundraising by fulfilling their need for specificity. An educational tool containing specific board fundraising activities is provided on page 22. This worksheet enables board members to choose from a wide variety of ways to support the organization's development program.

Turn to page 22 for **The BoardSource Fundraising Checklist.**

Giving Thanks

Finally, when the asking is done and the donation made, do not forget the importance of acknowledging the donor's generosity. The phrase "I can't thank you enough" is truer in fundraising than in any other part of life. Both donors and volunteers need to be thanked. Board members are among the most powerful of "thankers."

Provide your donors with recognition, appreciation, and steady communication about your work, and you set the stage for the next ask.

1.
The Board's Role in Fundraising

Among the various responsibilities of the board, none is more important than ensuring that the organization has adequate resources to remain financially viable. There is a fundamental distinction in this respect between the board, which decides to embark on fundraising programs, and the individual board members, who are ultimately charged with helping to execute that mission. In deciding that fundraising is necessary, the board is sending the message that its members agree to make commitments to help. There are various forms this commitment can take — not all have to be explicitly financial — but it is vital that all members of the board personally support the fundraising effort. This book explains the different ways to contribute, even for those who have never before participated in a fundraising campaign or sought solicitations.

PUTTING FUNDRAISING IN PERSPECTIVE

Board members often lament about being asked to raise funds for the organizations they serve. For the uninitiated, the task of fundraising may even come as a surprise. Even those who expect the request can find it daunting. When confronted with fundraising responsibilities, board members who are uncertain about their skills in this area may have a range of responses:

- "When I joined the board, no one told me I would have to raise money."

- "Why is fundraising a board responsibility?"

- "I give my time — isn't that enough?"

Although each concern is valid and deserves a response, *fundraising for most nonprofits is an integral part of board service.* Indeed, perhaps *the* most important duty. Because the organization requires money to fulfill its mission and ensure its future, fundraising is woven into the broader responsibilities of strategic planning and leadership. As the chief leadership body, the board has to accomplish three fundamental tasks:

Through *Stewardship* the board is ultimately accountable for the health and effectiveness of the enterprise.

By sustaining *Capacity* the board offers wisdom, oversees the organization's work, and attends to the foundations of its wealth.

In preserving *Credibility* the board brings the weight of the good will and generosity of the organization to the community.

Fundamental to delivering on these promises is the ability to raise the money that enables the organization to function. While board members who hadn't been led to understand in advance that they would be expected to raise funds might at first balk at the notion, it is imperative that anxieties be allayed and the importance of the mission underscored. When the importance of their fundraising effort is explained, few reluctant board members will balk at pitching in. The challenge is to embolden them to become fearless in their efforts.

BOARD COMMITMENT

Board members show their dedication in many ways. They can provide leadership and governance to an expanding organization, increase the organization's visibility in the community, identify partnerships beneficial to the organization, and provide valuable, necessary professional skills or insight. The list goes on. The point is that serving on a board involves a multitude of functions, some formal and some informal. The bottom line: Board members are the primary champions and supporters for all aspects of the organization — including fundraising.

Clarifying expectations from the start, when new members are being recruited, can ensure the board's participation in this important area of service. Before members join the board, they need to understand in detail what fundraising involvement is expected of them. Board members who admire an organization's mission and feel compassion for its clients or cause are prime candidates for being willing to share their time with the organization, to make financial contributions, and to solicit funds from others in its behalf.

It is particularly important that the board act unanimously in its display of commitment, for this lends invaluable strength to its solicitations to outside parties. The first step to becoming fearless is to be familiar with the kinds of development behavior that communicate commitment to outsiders:

- Understand the organization, its origins, and its needs.

- Be involved in the organization's fundraising program.

- Make personal monetary contributions.

Personal giving by those most closely associated with the organization lends vital credibility to its work in the eyes of others. Such credibility is an essential ingredient in any effort to raise money. Contributions by board members affirm that those closest to and most responsible for programs believe them worthy of support. The lack of significant personal giving by board members, on the other hand, can cripple appeals for financial assistance to others since potential donors are rightfully skeptical if board members themselves are not contributing.

Contributing also performs a psychological function; **it gives board members confidence to ask others to give.** This point needs to be emphasized, particularly for those whose nature is not naturally disposed to asking others for contributions. The satisfaction with your decision to make a donation yourself gives you a shot of confidence in your fundraising efforts seeking to persuade others to do likewise.

IMPROVING PARTICIPATION

How does a board go about achieving 100 percent member giving? How does it emphasize that a one-time gift is not enough and that increasing commitment is desirable?

The key is establishing clear expectations from the start.

Each board should have a profile of board membership responsibilities or a job description drafted by board members themselves, discussed fully, and accepted as the standard for membership. Such job descriptions are exceptionally helpful in defining expectations of prospective board members. Do not hurry this process of formulating the job description; if it takes a year to agree upon and to adopt the outline with a sense of ownership, it would be time well spent.

Obviously, one section of the board job description will outline board members' fundraising responsibilities. Usually those who agree to serve are already giving to one or more nonprofit organizations. Therefore, this component of the profile may read:

Members of this board are expected to include [name of organization] in their annual philanthropic giving at a level commensurate with their resources. Board members need not give equal amounts but must make an equal commitment toward helping the organization provide services.

The key word in the above description is *include.* Few board members would believe it an extreme imposition to dedicate a portion of their annual charitable gifts to the organization on whose board they serve.

Board members often ask, "*How much should I give?*" The following guidelines can help determine an appropriate amount to contribute.

- Give enough so you care how it's spent.

- Give what is of real value to you; it will then be of value to the organization.

- Give at a level that will enable you to join a donor club; in other words, a contribution in proportion to your financial capability.

BOARD DIVERSITY

Board composition plays an important role in an organization's ability to raise money. The broader it reaches out into different strata, the more opportunities for board members to solicit funds. In composing a board, it makes good sense to consider where the networks of prospective members extends. Obviously, influence and affluence are useful. However, even those without abundant financial means can become effective fundraisers, particularly if they bring a unique background and passion to their pursuit. Board members who are also clients and constituents of the organization can make for powerful fundraisers; by telling their personal stories, these individuals provide a real-life example of the organization's effectiveness and inspire contributions.

A diverse board links the organization with multiple constituents. Board members of different races, genders, backgrounds, professions, and ages serve as ambassadors to different communities.

All board members have individual talents, connections, and skills to tap. Voluntary organizations must build from these diverse starting points. Someday they may have multimillion dollar donors but at the outset it's wise to put such fantasies of never having to worry about money aside and recognize the importance of building strong fundraising capabilities in a variety of communities. Think of your board's fundraising potential like a diverse investment portfolio in which each member plays a unique role.

2.

Why Donors Give — And Why They Don't

A vital competency in becoming a fearless fundraiser is the ability to "read" prospective donors. Donors give for their own personal reasons. In approaching prospects, be attentive to what motivates them and not necessarily what the organization considers the rationale for giving. Giving is an exchange transaction. Consciously or not, people give to get something (even when they consider themselves being altruistic). It can be a lot of things: satisfaction, closure, relief from guilt, or other benefits. Tax considerations may influence the amount or timing of a gift. Keep your ears open when you're talking to prospects; *hear* what they tell you about their motivation.

A persuasive way to open a conversation is to emphasize that a contribution should be regarded as an **investment** in a charitable organization; the work it does in the community is the dividend. Consequently, asking for gifts opens the door for the donor to accomplish something in concert with others that individually could not be achieved. It sustains collective action, action capable of important accomplishments.

I want to be remembered for more than a tombstone on some grassy knoll was the emphatic way one donor prospect described his ambition. To such a person, the act of giving money can be presented as the ultimate empowerment. In motivating others to give, the appeal to this kind of collective enterprise is a powerful motivator. Appreciating the true nature of philanthropy allows board members to develop a more positive outlook and even consider new personal initiatives.

WHAT MOTIVATES A DONOR?

Although each donor has specific reasons for making a gift, there are common themes. Knowing these reasons for giving can help board members be more persuasive in framing appeals. By identifying what's important to the prospective donor and structuring the appeal around those issues, the experience becomes more fulfilling and satisfying for the fundraiser as well since it revolves around subjects the prospect cares about.

Below are some reasons donors give.

- They want to make a difference.
- They are sharing their good fortune.
- Their beliefs are being expressed in a tangible way.
- They want to invest in a worthy cause.
- They are demonstrating their commitment.
- Someone they respect sent them an invitation.
- Others they know and trust are also contributing.
- They are seeking an opportunity to change the status quo.
- They want to associate themselves with the reputation of the organization.
- By donating to a public charity, they are deriving tax benefits.

WHEN DO DONORS GIVE?

Timing plays an important role in the donor decision. The elements that make up this timing often have a large emotional and psychological component. Not until prospective donors feel secure in their judgment are they likely to pull the trigger and write a check. When do people give? They give when they feel inspired to do so. In framing a solicitation, be alert to this inspiration factor.

These are some factors that help tip a prospective donor's emotional balance sheet in favor of contribution:

- They are involved in the organization or cause.
- Representatives from the organization really listen to them.
- Compassion is stirred and heart strings are touched.
- They are confident that contributions are used wisely and with care.
- Someone they know and respect asks them to give.
- They are clear that their gift will help the organization accomplish objectives they care about.
- They understand that their gift will really make a difference.
- They wish to pay tribute to someone through a charitable contribution (in appreciation for, in honor of, or in memory of a particular person or event).

- They support the mission and want it to move forward.

- Someone they trust explains the urgency of the need.

- They receive appropriate recognition for their gift.

- They feel good donating to a deserving charity that produces results.

- They want to pay a personal debt, such as contributing to an organization that helped them through an illness or other crisis.

WHY DO PROSPECTS FAIL TO GIVE?

To be a fearless fundraiser, it is important to have tough skin. Remember, don't take rejection personally. There are lots of reasons why a solicitation fails and most of them have nothing to do with you. A declining stock market, for example, will influence donor behavior and it's a factor you can't control. The important thing is to be armed with knowledge of the potential pitfalls that you *can* influence and to take action to address them. Luck, as they say, is the residue of design.

People fail to give for numerous reasons:

- Solicitation was infrequent or ineffective.

- Information was lacking about the difference their gift made.

- They never felt wanted or needed.

- The organization did not ask their opinions or include them in plans or programs.

- They received no direct, personalized appeal by someone excited about the organization's accomplishments.

- No one asked them to give again, to consider giving more, or to help find others to give.

- A previous gift went unacknowledged.

Last but not least, as every sales person knows, ***you've got to ask for the sale!*** Don't be too timid to make the request for a contribution. The people whom a board member is soliciting are, for some reason, in a position where they're likely to be willing and able to give. They *want* to give but not if nobody asks.

To summarize with the dictum most fundamental of all fundraising precepts: People give to people. But people are more likely to give to those they hold in high esteem, to individuals they know have already donated themselves, and to those whose convictions have prompted them to directly ask for a pledge or a gift. This scenario constitutes healthy peer pressure and is by far the most powerful fundraising technique.

TRY THIS!

Get Inside a Donor's Head

Understanding the donor mindset is important. To help understand how to motivate others, *ask yourself why you give to charity*. Write down the charities to which you donate regularly and describe the primary reasons that you do so. Share the reasons with other board members. By acknowledging and understanding your own personal motivations, you will become better at asking for gifts.

3.

Motivating a Fearless Fundraiser

OVERCOMING FEAR OF FAILURE

Fear of failure is the universal hurdle that anybody in a solicitation role must overcome. Board members asked to go out and raise funds from friends, colleagues and contacts are particularly subject to being intimidated by fear of failure to the point where they are embarrassed to take the critical step of scheduling a face-to-face meeting for fear of being turned down. What many board members don't realize is that in-person solicitation is the most successful fundraising method, ranking well above any other method — bulk-rate mail, personalized letters, telephone calls. And, in contrast to those other methods, it's considerably less costly. So in building up your courage to schedule that first meeting to request donations, remember that this is *the most cost-efficient solicitation mode that your organization can employ.*

Personal interaction also provides an opportunity to spread the word about your organization, to do public relations and image building and constituent development. Even if your prospects aren't ready to whip out the checkbook, they've learned more about the organization and shared some of your passion.

Seeking direct contact also allows you to *qualify* prospects. Remember, if prospects aren't at all interested in your cause, they won't take a meeting; but if they *do* agree to see you face to face, they've already declared their interest. Future resources, particularly more costly ones, will be focused on these qualified prospects. **So even if somebody says "no" when you request a meeting, you've accomplished a productive list management task, which will enhance the long-range organizational fundraising process.**

"No" may mean many different things, but — to repeat what all accomplished sales folks understand — rarely is it a personal rejection. "No" may mean not now, not yet, not for that amount, not in cash, not for this program, or not until I feel more comfortable. When you take the risk, make the request and hear "no," don't despair. Don't flee the conversation in embarrassment. On the contrary, keep it going. Find out what kind of "no" the prospect is expressing. If volunteers do not take risks and make some errors, they have no chance to learn or grow. Fear is expensive! It can prevent you from finding and winning supporters.

Solicitations involve negotiation. Don't expect a positive response right away. Give prospects time to think. Here are a few sample questions to ask, which show you how to facilitate the productive give-and-take that can eventually lead to contribution.

- "$200 might be too much. Would you consider $150?"

- "Will you pledge that amount over a two-year period? Three?"

- "Are you willing to reconsider your answer? We could talk about it more next week."

- "Under what conditions would you consider making a gift?"

- "What would change your mind about this program?"

- "We understand why you might not be able to give right now but could you give us the names of several friends who might be interested?"

- "We have other giving options that might be more convenient for you. Can I return to discuss some of them?"

- "We really appreciate the issues you've raised. I'm going to return to my organization to discuss them. Then can we schedule another meeting with you for me to present our results?"

TRY THIS!

Practicing the "Ask"

Role playing is one proven approach to increase fundraising skills. During role-playing exercises, board members can explore several appropriate ways to ask for a donation, including some of the following examples.

- "Will you consider a pledge of $___ for the purpose of. . .?"

- "We have already received $___; will you join your peers by giving a gift of $___?"

- "Please consider joining me in meeting the needs of [name the program]. Your gift will help us extend our services."

- "I'd like to ask you to put us in your contribution budget this year."

- "We have various giving plans. How would you like to participate?"

- "Would you consider what you gave last year as the first installment on a three-year pledge? It would mean a great deal to this campaign."

- "Your gift of $___ would have a significant impact and lead others to follow your example."

4.

Understanding the Nature of Charitable Giving

Not every member of a voluntary board intuitively comprehends the rationale for charitable contributions. Understanding of the nature of charitable giving, however, is indispensable to a board member's ability to raise money. Philanthropy is not a strange or foreign concept, but a basic dimension of our democratic heritage.

Board members who understand the value of nonprofit organizations in general and the specific role that their organization fills, stand head and shoulders above the pack as convincing advocates. To ensure that board members are conversant with this aspect of the role of philanthropy in a democracy, it is advisable prior to ongoing fundraising that there be a presentation made at a board meeting. A carefully planned discussion will help board members understand philanthropy in this context. Handouts, articles, or human-interest stories and occasional individual testimonials from clients, staff, or other volunteers can increase the board's awareness of the urgency of charitable donations.

THE MOST POWERFUL APPEAL: CHARITABLE GIFTS AS INVESTMENTS

A common misconception among novice fundraisers is that asking people to give money to charity is asking them to give it away. This is not the case. *Charitable gifts are investments.* Not only do charitable gifts help improve the quality of life for others, donors themselves receive a benefit from their donation. As Kay Sprinkel Grace, a noted fundraising consultant and author, reminds us: "Toss out the tin cup." Soliciting voluntary gifts is not begging, and "ask" is not a four-letter word. Requesting people to donate money to a charitable cause is not an unnatural act. Nor is it illegal or uncouth. Asking someone to support a worthy cause is not a put-down or a social faux pas. On the contrary, it affords prospects a friendly, totally voluntary opportunity to contribute to a noble mission or to help fulfill a pressing social need.

EMPLOYING THE STAFF AS A RESOURCE

What is the role of the staff in fundraising? There are many opportunities for staff involvement to facilitate the development of a cadre of fearless fundraisers. Determine whether your organization's staff or board members handle the tasks listed below. These three lists may help initiate a discussion of the different roles in fundraising (and indicate whether or not your organization is arranged for optimal fundraising effectiveness).

The staff's role in fundraising is listed below.

- Help identify prospects.

- Initiate and generate ideas and draft policies.

- Keep files, records, and mailing lists.

- Manage the acknowledgment process.

- Conduct research.

- Prepare correspondence.

- Write proposals and reports.

- Assist volunteer leaders in cultivation and selected solicitation activities.

The board's role in fundraising is listed below.

- Define the mission and plan for the future.

- Support organizational stability.

- Identify strong leadership.

- Support and approve adequate budgets.

- Participate in a variety of ways.

As the process ensues, a natural synergy evolves between an enlightened board and a smoothly functioning, well-led staff. The fruits of this relationship support fearless fundraising with a foundation of contacts, support materials, and implementation follow-up.

The seamless interface of board and staff in fundraising accomplishes the following:

- Background information and suggestions help shape the board's fundraising policies.

- Development of basic arguments show why donors should contribute to the organization.

- Strong relationships with prospects are stronger.

CONNECTING FUNDRAISING TO PROGRAMS

Why do board members raise money? So that the organization's important programs and services can continue. In developing annual fundraising programs, goals should be explicitly tied to the budget. *Another way to be fearless is to focus not on the request for money but rather the mission you are seeking to implement.* When board members see the relationship between how much money they need to raise and the organization's ability to accomplish its mission, the task of fundraising takes on greater clarity.

SUPPORT FROM MANY FRONTS

An organization's revenues are more stable if they come from multiple, diverse sources rather than a single source. For instance, consider a small, nonprofit social service organization that receives 60 percent of its annual operating budget from a single federal program. If Congress decides to eliminate that program, the nonprofit is crippled by the immediate loss of more than half its budget. However, if the organization has an active fundraising program that provides a broad base of community support from individuals, foundations, and corporations, the loss of a single revenue stream will not diminish the organization's ability to function. This is another motivator that keeps the fearless fundraiser going — the knowledge that more is better, not just in terms of total dollar amount, but by propping up the base of the organization with a foundation strong enough to withstand shock waves.

TRY THIS!

Learning over the Long Term

Create an instruction manual about what a board member needs to know in order to sustain fundraising efforts over a long period. By breaking basic fundraising instruction into manageable pieces, organizations can help board members digest the information more readily before they move on to more advanced instruction. List the 10 most important lessons that your organization has learned about how it raises funds. Then order them into sequential order — which of the lessons happens first, second, third, etc. Ask the staff to suggest what they could do to lend support at each stage in the process. Don't try to make this into a final, perfect model but rather try quickly to produce a first draft.

As the wise elder explained to the young warrior fearful that he would be unable to accomplish the monumental task he had been given, "Take it one step at a time."

5.

Acquiring the Tools You Need To Be a Fearless Fundraiser

After inculcating a winning attitude, the next step in turning board members into fearless fundraisers is to provide them with some specialized training in organizational development.

Organizations can use the chart on page 16 to assess individual board members' experience, support needs, and possible training.

- In Box 1, list board members who have little or no knowledge of fundraising techniques, and have never been asked to participate in the development process.

- In Box 2, list board members who understand how to do it, but have not been active on behalf of your organization.

- In Box 3, list board members who have had no training in fundraising, but have been willing to do it in the past.

- In Box 4, list those who both know how to raise funds and have been willing to do it.

Board members in Box 1 need to learn techniques and practice.

Board members in Box 2 require an assessment to determine why they have not been active in fundraising. Has nobody asked them? Have they been asked but been unwilling to take on assignments? What is the impact of this group on the rest of the board?

Board members in Box 3 are to be thanked and cherished. They are naturals. There may be new fundraising strategies such as those listed in this book that they could learn and help implement. At a minimum, they should be asked to be mentors to those just starting out.

Board members in Box 4 are the workhorses of any fundraising program. They need thanks, support, and as many opportunities to lead as possible.

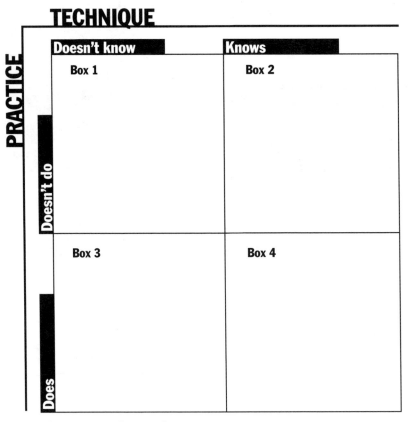

TECHNIQUE

	Doesn't know	Knows
Doesn't do	Box 1	Box 2
Does	Box 3	Box 4

(left axis label: **PRACTICE**)

The goal is to move the members in Box 1 into Box 4.

Preparing board members to raise funds is the first stage in moving each member closer toward Box 4. Before they can venture out into the community to solicit donors, board members must prepare a case statement. What is the case? The case is a compelling statement of values the organization endorses and impact it exerts. This case study formalizes the workings of your organization so prospective donors quickly understand why they want to make their contributions.

Build your case statement from the donor's perspective:

1. Describe the organization through the eyes of a donor, not through the internal workings of the organization. What do you want an outsider looking in to see? What is the mission of the organization that will most appeal to outsiders? How do people who work in the organization serve their mission? What are the clients like; how do the benefits they receive endorse the mission?

2. Remember that *people give money to make a change for the good,* not to support an organization. Donors have their own concerns and ego needs. The case statement should stress how the donation makes a difference because of the benefits it confers.

3. Position the donation as a personal investment. The people you are approaching are comfortable with the notion of investing their money. What they expect from these investments is a return. Explain the accruing impact a donation will have over the years and how benefits will compound over time.

To make your case, you need to have good answers to these questions:

What — What need does the organization fulfill?

How — How is the organization meeting this need?

Who — Who is the organization — its leadership, its record, its mission?

Why — Why should the donor contribute?

After having answered these questions, you could be ready to summarize all the elements of your case statement into a succinct, coherent, emotionally persuasive position statement. It all comes down to the bottom line: What will be the return on the donor's gift?

KNOW THE MAJOR SOURCES OF FUNDING

Contributions come from a variety of sources. Among the sources of contributions are

- governments

- foundations

- businesses and corporations

- nonprofit institutions, associations, and religious organizations

- individuals

(As an exercise, list several possible donors in each category for you to approach. Think creatively. Imagine unlikely possibilities.)

TRY THIS!

Know Your Elevator Speech

Imagine that you are stuck in an elevator with one other person. As you commiserate with each other, you learn that she directs one of the larger corporate giving programs in the community. When she asks you about yourself, you decide to get her interested in the organization you serve. Time is limited but you realize this is an extraordinary opportunity to do some fearless fundraising. What are the three or four points you want to share with her about the organization? Write down several sentences, which will allow you to introduce each point and launch a conversation.

COMMITTING RESOURCES TO EMPOWER BOARD MEMBERS TO BE FEARLESS FUNDRAISERS

One reason many boards hesitate to spend sufficient amounts of money on fundraising activities is that they fail to realize the potential returns of fundraising investments. Expenditures for fundraising are usually high-yield investments. For instance, assume that the board has $10,000 to invest. It can place the money in a bond that yields four percent and at the end of the year it will have $10,400. Year two, it will have $10,816. Year three, $11,232 and so forth. Alternatively, it can spend the $10,000 on a systematic annual giving campaign that produces, let's say for example, 50 donations of $500 over the same three years. The value of that $10,000 has now grown to $25,000.

Where else can an organization get such a high return? Board members are often stunned to hear an example such as this one — sometimes so much so that they immediately want to discuss budget revisions to increase the amount spent on fundraising.

BOARD PREPARATION

Is your board ready to engage in fundraising activities? Before you tackle your individual situations, consider the following questions:

- Is your board ready to adopt a plan of action?

- Is a sound strategic plan in place?

- Is the board roster complete?

- Is strong board leadership in place?

- Are board members attending meetings regularly?

- Are board members completing assignments?

- Has each board member made a personal donation?

- Is staff support available to assist in the board's efforts?

6.

The Fearless Fundraiser Development Worksheet

GUIDE BOARD MEMBERS TO MORE SUCCESSFUL FUNDRAISING

All board members need some background about the development process before they can begin to raise money. They need to know the who, what, why, and how of fundraising. After they have a base of knowledge, board members understand how each of them can make a difference as individuals.

This section of this book provides a hands-on checklist designed to encourage board members to become fearless in their fundraising pursuits by providing an array of opportunities — enough choices for every board member's tastes and preferences.

Tested in workshops and presentations, this approach eases anxieties and fears about fundraising by providing a step-by-step approach that moves members ever closer to Box 4. These specific fundraising activities provide board members with tactics that ease them from one stage of effectiveness to the next. This approach works because it is concrete. It outlines a wide range of options suited to different personalities and comfort zones, each building in a programmatic way to develop a more inclusive, coherent, fearless fundraiser.

Any size nonprofit, from grassroots groups to well-established institutions, can benefit from this approach. It embodies a variety of the fundraising strategies combined into a single program.

There are three levels to this worksheet, reflecting different degrees of board member expertise and comfort level in fundraising.

LEVEL ONE: BUILDING THE FOUNDATION

Level One demands little personal risk. This most basic level involves activities the board accomplishes as a group, such as setting strategic fundraising goals and deciding priorities. Level One activities are basic to the process and without them donor cultivation and solicitation is not always successful.

It's critical to establish and fine-tune the fundraising plan and rationale for support. Only organized activity rooted in agreed-upon objectives can be effective in the long run. The strategic activities found in Level One allow board members to start slowly, build on their understanding, and become more comfortable with the process.

LEVEL TWO: GATHERING MOMENTUM THROUGH "FRIEND RAISING"

Level Two outlines numerous ways board members can support prospect cultivation and outreach. For some board members, Level Two activities will stretch both their vision and capabilities, making their service more productive.

Activities outlined in Level Two guide board members to understand the essential role of relationship building with prospective donors. This is the start of "Friend Raising." Board members help donors and prospects learn more about the program as they share their conviction about its mission and services.

Special events are a type of Level Two activity. They heighten interest, draw in volunteers, and give the cause visibility. And they can be fun! Special events do not replace more direct methods of fundraising but they do provide a perfect opportunity to cultivate prospects.

LEVEL THREE: COMMITMENT AND SOLICITATION

Level Three focuses on the sensitive topics of personal giving and asking others for monetary gifts. Focused relationship building, as a prelude to making "the ask," is an important part of Level Three's action guidelines. Experts agree that time, talent, and treasure — or work, wisdom, and wealth — are all needed for effective fundraising. None of these substitutes for the others.

Level Three activities are the most difficult to initiate. It is advisable for the board to work as a group to break down understandable resistance individuals may display as they develop into fearless fundraisers comfortable making the request for money.

Board members should think of each one-on-one solicitation as a continuation of their training. Even unsuccessful solicitations can be useful. By listening actively and being open to what prospective donors say, board members can fine-tune their approach and learn how to better solicit a donor the next time. Fundraising is not "all or nothing."

TRY THIS!

Fundraising: It's in the Cards

This simple exercise provides one way to increase the performance of board members in Level Three activities. Print out basic data for selected prospects or lapsed donors on index cards and arrange them alphabetically on a table. As members enter the room, invite them to scan the names and pick up five or six. Write a sample script tailored to the details on each card — how would you approach the person, present the case for the organization, seek an appointment, solicit a donation. Then exchange cards with another member of the board. Both of you do the same exercise with the other's cards. Then compare. Learn from each other's approach. Remember, there's no single right approach. Any method is acceptable — as long as it involves making the ask.

When preparing for an "ask," remember

- Practice your presentation.

- Misery loves company — go with a partner.

- Have an amount in mind.

- Use inviting language.

- Focus on the worthiness of the cause.

THE BOARDSOURCE FUNDRAISING CHECKLIST

FUNDRAISING RESPONSIBILITIES AND OPPORTUNITIES FOR NONPROFIT BOARD MEMBERS

This inventory offers several benefits. First, it expands the notion of fundraising to include many activities other than asking for donations. It also solicits concrete information from individual board members about which tasks they are willing to complete. Finally, it provides a snapshot of the board's self-confidence and capacity, allowing the staff to provide customized support materials.

Be honest. Be realistic. Be willing to try something new.

How many are YOU willing to consider and undertake?

Mark each: *Y* = **YES** *N* = **NO** *M* = **MAYBE (No more than 10 Maybes)**

Level One: Building The Foundation

____ 1. **Commit** to the organization's vision and mission. Be willing to learn more about how to give and get contributed resources.

____ 2. **Provide** informed input into a market-oriented planning process (help decide which goals deserve priority given organizational capabilities, resources, depth of volunteer commitment, and implementation strategies).

____ 3. **Aid** in the creation of the fund development plan. Understand the plan's implications. Be willing to help execute it. (If you cannot, state why this is and be willing to work toward consensus on some revisions.)

____ 4. **Assist** in drafting the fundraising case statement — a comprehensive justification for charitable support — and be able to explain this rationale persuasively.

____ 5. **Decide** realistic budget allocations for the organization's fundraising program. (Be patient about how fast new income will be received, but ask questions, offer suggestions, and operate by agreed-upon procedures and assignments.)

____ 6. **Review, critique, and monitor** the action strategy — a policy and procedure outline of how and when the program is to be implemented. (This could be about types of fundraising on which to concentrate, methods of approach, ways to identify target markets, or how gifts are to be sought, allocated, reported, acknowledged, and then leveraged for more along with specific benchmarks to measure outcomes.)

_____ 7. **Understand** the organization's financial situation and probable future funding position. (Resist quick fixes and short-range decisions. Probe until you become convinced money is wisely used and staff is accountable.)

_____ 8. **Evaluate** progress by asking friendly — but searching — questions. (Are we doing what we agreed to do?) If no, why not? Are we getting improved results as time goes on? What specifically? If no, why? What reasonable changes might be explored? What do we require that is not available currently? Expertise? Staff time? Volunteers? Commitment level?)

_____ 9. **Join and get active** on at least one board committee and be alert for how its work can strengthen current fundraising endeavors. (Almost every aspect of the operation has some impact on development, directly or indirectly.)

_____ 10. **Approve** the creation or revision of a board member statement of responsibilities that includes clearly defined expectations for their personal giving and involvement in fundraising.

Level Two: "Friend Raising"

_____ 11. **Provide** the names and addresses of donor prospects for the development mailing list. (Share pertinent information about your contacts: individual preferences, interest level, any misgivings about the cause, and their inclination to donate money.)

_____ 12. **Research** phone numbers or secure exact addresses for campaign mailings.

_____ 13. **Attend** training workshop(s) to discover how better to carry out your role and to augment the overall development process.

_____ 14. **Prepare** useful and informative training materials for board members and other volunteers about how to raise funds.

_____ 15. **Recruit** volunteers and prospective helpers and suggest ways to interest and to involve persons with whom you or your friends are acquainted.

_____ 16. **Advocate** for the organization or cause and serve as an enthusiastic community relations representative. (Understand the organization's mission and programs and be prepared to answer common questions. Prompt others in the community to begin participating in the work of the organization.)

_____ 17. **Acquire** mailing lists from a variety of sources in the community to augment the organization's database.

_____ 18. **Facilitate** introductions and access to individuals or groups where you have credibility and influence. Nurture prospects and donors on a regular basis.

_____ 19. **Distribute** (hand deliver) invitations or promotional material to targeted markets: individuals, businesses, churches, temples, community groups, or clubs.

_____ 20. **Cultivate** more varied media contacts for wider publicity and promotion. Link your organization with regional councils, societies, or associations. Seek out wider sponsorship for events, programs, or educational sessions.

_____ 21. **Join** the speakers bureau or agree to be a spokesperson for your organization at some specific occasion or event.

_____ 22. **Spearhead** the formation of a business and professional advisory group and encourage one of your own professional advisors (such as a CPA or an attorney) to become involved.

_____ 23. **Find and relate** one or more human-interest stories to illustrate why gifts are needed and how they are used to provide, enhance, or expand your organization's outreach and impact.

_____ 24. **Brainstorm** innovative ways to thank and to recognize donors. For instance, arrange a special "thank-a-thon" in which board members phone donors to express gratitude for their contributions, with no solicitation included in the conversation.

_____ 25. **Research** individual prospects, foundations, and corporate funding sources through public information sources. Locate promotional partners or establish a joint venture. Summarize your findings for staff or committee use.

_____ 26. **Write** a personal testimonial or letter of support for public use or agree to be quoted as to why you support the organization.

_____ 27. **Hand-deliver** thank-yous, acknowledgments, or special awards to volunteers, contributors, or support groups.

_____ 28. **Participate** in an evaluation session, during which you help campaign leaders gather the information they need about giving patterns and capacity of identified prospects.

_____ 29. **Assist** in fundraising special events, such as auctions, fairs, bazaars, open houses, tours, or tournaments. Enlist others to help in ways that they perceive are useful and fun, so they will want to do it again. Welcome newcomers; circulate and mingle to spread a friendly spirit, learn names, and discover common interests.

_____ 30. **Sell** products, tickets, or premiums where proceeds directly benefit your organization.

_____ 31. **Visit** a community leader to explain needs to be met and accomplishments of the organization. Initiate follow-up visits to sustain and increase interest.

_____ 32. **Host** — in your home or at a restaurant — a small group of volunteers or donor prospects to better acquaint them with the value of your organization's priorities: educational programs, advancement of a cause, or effective human-services delivery.

_____ 33. **Establish** a planned giving program by finding ways to underline the importance of a remember-us-in-your-will emphasis.

Level Three: Solicitation

_____ 34. **Contact** local businesses and vendor suppliers to seek an in-kind donation, such as supplies, equipment, technical assistance, or personnel (interns, released time, loaned executives, etc.).

_____ 35. **Personalize** the annual direct mail program or other endorsed campaign by using at least two of the following techniques:

- Hand address envelopes for use with top donors.

- Add a personal P. S. or thank-you on the prepared acknowledgment.

- Compose and send your note of appreciation for a gift.

- Phone to thank some of those who responded.

_____ 36. **Increase** your donation each year to help reach the goal and assist in setting the pace for others, so that you will become a credible solicitor.

_____ 37. **Request** a pledge or a contribution from designated prospects or lapsed donors.

_____ 38. **Solicit** a cash contribution from a service club, civic group, or church or temple, or request a gift for a particular promotion or publication.

_____ 39. **Accept** a leadership role to organize solicitation teams or a specific campaign.

_____ 40. **Ask** selected individuals for a specific gift or a multiyear pledge. Visit them personally, accompanied by a staff member or another volunteer.

How To Use The Fearless Fundraiser Development Worksheet

After analyzing your individual response, the results of your fellow board members can be tallied together and used to address the performance of the board as a whole.

We recommend this conversation occur within the context of a specially designated board meeting. Introducing and discussing concrete development activities are positive steps toward board members becoming more meaningfully involved in fundraising. More board members will be inspired to make bolder, more fearless fundraising calls.

To stimulate discussion

As a discussion draft, the results tally can stimulate discussion about new ways the board and staff can work together to improve fundraising results. Arrange for a few members to comment on specific items, pro or con, so that the meeting moves beyond generalities. Address each section in turn.

At a board retreat

Set aside time at a retreat or extended board session for all members to complete the worksheet. Interpret and discuss individual results and the collective response of your board as a whole.

In small groups

Divide the board into three groups and assign each group a specific Level of activity to analyze and evaluate. Groups can rank the items in order of preference. As the small groups report their results, they can share their opinions and reservations about the activities. Open discussion facilitates the constructive handling of controversial subjects.

As a model action plan

Extract selected points from Levels Two and Three and use them to stimulate a brainstorming session. During the session, board members can decide how to customize these activities to their organization. For instance, the board may decide to integrate items from the checklist into their own formal job descriptions.

Conclusion

Confidence is vital for developing your fundraising potential. Such confidence arises out of a commitment to the cause, knowledge that all board members contribute, and understanding the organization's programs. Dedication emerges from the conviction that fundraising efforts will help meet needs, close gaps, solve problems, or aid an underserved, vulnerable group.

While no development activity is easy, the checklist of concrete fundraising action steps can help board members get started. With plenty of choices, the checklist enables every board member to select at least a few. This instrument helps clear up the mystery of fundraising, taking into account differing levels of ability, experience, and interest among volunteers.

Discussing the checklist will evoke changes in the way involvement in fundraising is considered. Even if only a few board members "catch fire," they can enthusiastically lead the way for the many who shy away from participation. Board members who follow this process seriously will then be able to respond fearlessly to the summons: "Will you help us raise money?"

Appendix I

FOUNDATION AND FUNDRAISING RESOURCES

The following list provides additional references on funding and fundraising resources.

Association of Fundraising Professionals

The Association of Fundraising Professionals (AFP) is the professional association for individuals responsible for generating philanthropic support for a wide variety of charitable organizations. For members, AFP's fundraising resource center is free. Learn more at www.afpnet.org.

BoardSource

BoardSource has several booklets, books, and videos on fundraising. Learn more at www.boardsource.org or call 800-883-6262.

The Council on Foundations

The Council on Foundations is a membership association of grantmaking foundations and corporate giving programs. Its mission is to promote responsible and effective philanthropy by assisting foundations in achieving their goals. Visit www.cof.org to find the locations of member foundations. Numerous links offer information about specific foundations and their programs. Contact the Council by phone at 202-466-6512; or by mail at 1828 L Street, NW, 3rd Floor, Washington, DC 20036.

The Foundation Center

The Foundation Center serves the information needs of grantmakers and grantseekers by offering a variety of programs on fundraising. It is an excellent resource for locating grantmakers and learning to write successful proposals. Five libraries in New York, Washington, D.C., Atlanta, San Francisco, and Cleveland are open to the public. Access the virtual center at www.fdncenter.org. The Foundation Center has an extensive publications catalog and it organizes regular workshops on this topic.

Federal Grants

Numerous federal grants are available for nonprofits. When seeking federal funding, it is helpful to learn the types of grants available (cooperative agreements, block grants, closed-end grants, open-end grants, discretionary grants, and mandatory grants); the application procedure; and your obligations upon receiving a grant. Check following resources:

The *Federal Register*: the official newspaper for the federal government, updated daily; visit www.federalregisterdigest.com.

National and state agencies: directly contact agencies that are applicable to your project or mission and find out what is available.

Research Grants

The Aspen Institute: The Institute operates the Nonprofit Sector Research Fund, which supports outstanding basic and applied research on nonprofit organizations. Learn more at www.aspeninst.org.

Internet Fundraising Resources

The Internet provides ample information on fundraising and available grants. More and more organizations are preparing their own Web sites to function as fundraisers. The article, "How Can We Use the Internet for Fundraising?" addresses many of the issues involved in Internet fundraising: www.nonprofit-info.org/misc/981027em.html.

Newspapers and Periodicals

These publications regularly run stories about fundraising and funding opportunities.

Contributions magazine: www.contributionsmagazine.com

Foundation News & Commentary: www.foundationnews.org

The Chronicle of Philanthropy: www.philanthropy.com

The NonProfit Times: www.nptimes.com

Appendix II

RESOURCES

Donovan, James A. *Take the Fear Out of Asking for Major Gifts*. Winter Park, FL: Donovan Management, Inc., 1993. This manual provides very specific treatment of the solicitation process with step-by-step instructions, self-study exercises, checklists, and charts, making it especially useful for training.

Drucker, Peter F. *Managing the Non-Profit Organization: Principles and Practices*. New York: Harper, 1992. Although it contains few specifics, this volume is absolutely basic for helping both staff and board understand the unique context and challenges of nonprofit organizations and why efficient and effective performance is essential for charitable support.

George, G. Worth. "What Part of No Don't You Understand?" Garden City, NY: Hoke Communications, *Fund Raising Management*, August 1992, pp. 38–41. This article spells out the variety of meanings a perceived turn-down may have, thus reassuring solicitors to continue their negotiations to elicit affirmative responses.

Grace, Kay Sprinkel. *Beyond Fundraising: New Strategies for Nonprofit Innovation and Investment*. New York: John Wiley & Sons, Inc., 1997. With an emphasis on development's relationship-building and values-based functions, this book presents theory and strategies for strengthening fundraising, board development, and planning in nonprofits.

Grant Thornton LLP. *Planned Giving: A Board Member's Perspective*. Washington, DC: BoardSource and Grant Thornton LLP., 1999. Written in clear terms, this book explains the different giving options available to donors. Board members will learn about present and deferred gifts, bequests, charitable trusts, and annuities. Use it to find out if planned giving is right for your organization and your donor base.

Herman, Robert D., and Heimovics, Richard D. *Executive Leadership in Nonprofit Organizations: New Strategies for Shaping Executive-Board Dynamics*. San Francisco: Jossey-Bass, 1991. An insightful treatment of this necessary partnership, this book emphasizes the strategic importance of the "leadership centrality of the chief executive" in relation to the "formal, hierarchical superiority" of the organization's board of directors.

Houle, Cyril O. *Governing Boards: Their Nature and Nurture*. Edited by Alan Shrader. San Francisco: Jossey-Bass, 1997. This classic volume about nonprofit directorship outlines the structure and functioning of a board and what shared responsibilities with staff involves.

Howe, Fisher. *The Board Member's Guide to Fund Raising*. San Francisco: Jossey-Bass, 1991. Living up to its title, this book offers a coherent foundation and also clear, practical steps to lead directors toward doing their part to implement development objectives.

Howe, Fisher. *Fund-Raising and the Nonprofit Board*. Washington, DC: BoardSource, 1998.This book outlines the five principles each board member should understand so that the full board can carry out its responsibility to raise funds.

Klein, Kim. *Fundraising for Social Change*. 4th ed., Berkeley, CA: Chardon Press, 2001. Especially relevant for smaller and grassroots organizations, the author explains both why fundraising is important and how to accomplish it.

Lansdowne, David. *Fund Raising Realities Every Board Member Must Face*. Medfield, MA: Emerson & Church, 1996. This book's subtitle may not do justice to this slim volume from which all trustees could derive some benefit. It summarizes a fearless approach to development activities: "A One-Hour Crash Course on Raising Major Gifts."

Nichols, Judith E. *Growing from Good to Great: Positioning Your Fund-Raising Efforts for Big Gains*. Chicago: Bonus Books, 1995. The author discusses how to reorganize fundraising to meet the challenge of demographic changes and includes a chapter on developing a board's fundraising strengths as a key aspect of positioning a nonprofit for major gains.

Panas, Jerold. *Boardroom Verities*. Chicago: Precept Press, 1998. This summary of 89 basic principles and tidbits discusses what works and what doesn't in achieving disciplined board results.

Rosso, Henry A. & Associates. *Achieving Excellence in Fund Raising*. San Francisco: Jossey-Bass, 1991. A compilation of 23 essays, this volume presents a comprehensive picture of fund development, including the role of trustees.

Seiler, Timothy L., and Grace, Kay Sprinkel, eds. *Achieving Trustee Involvement in Fundraising*. San Francisco: Jossey-Bass, 1994. This scholarly monograph maintains a consistent focus on the title theme. Especially pertinent is the discussion of building effective fundraising teams consisting of trustees and staff.

Speaking of Money: A Guide to Fund-Raising for Nonprofit Board Members. Washington, DC: BoardSource. Hosted by Hugh Downs, 1996. ABC News journalist Hugh Downs walks viewers through a series of candid interviews in which real board members explain why fundraising is an essential board responsibility, how board members work in partnership with staff, and how to ask for a gift. Equally suitable for use at board orientation sessions, development committee meetings, or board retreats, *Speaking of Money* is a thoughtful, inspiring, and humorous look at a critical board responsibility.

About the Author

Worth George served for 25 years as executive director of Pilgrim Place in Claremont, California, a nationally recognized community for retired church professionals. During his leadership, over $29 million was raised. A CFRE emeritus, he was president of the Inland chapter of the Association of Fundraising Professionals and was selected as Fundraiser of the Year in 1997. He earned two master's degrees, is included in *Who's Who in the West*, and has held state licenses in long-term care administration and personal counseling. Mr. George taught three separate courses in the University of San Francisco's Master of Nonprofit Administration program and is now a faculty member in Chapman University's award-winning Organizational Leadership master's sequence.